T4-APV-327

Copyright © 1963

THE ECONOMICS PRESS, INC.

West Orange, New Jersey

All Rights Reserved

Printed in U.S.A.

"UNACCUSTOMED AS I AM..."

An Executive's Guide to Public Speaking
by ARTHUR J. ZITO
Illustrated by Ted Key

PREFACE

THIS IS A LITTLE BOOK—*purposely so*. It contains everything you need to know in order to become an excellent public speaker. It contains very little you don't need to know—the text has not been padded or extended in any way to build up the size of the book.

It's a practical book for practical people. The author, Arthur J. Zito, is an experienced business executive as well as an excellent speaker. He reports the techniques he has used—and heard other expert speakers use—in all the various situations in which an executive may be called upon to take the floor and say something.

These techniques will work for you just the same as they do for the experts. The more experience you have had in public speaking the more you will recognize their soundness.

THE EDITORS

CONTENTS

SPEAKING FRANKLY . . .

WHAT KIND OF A SPEAKER are you? Can you stand in a meeting and effectively express your ideas? Can you sway an audience toward your point of view?

"Well—" some executives modestly begin, "I don't know how good I am, but I *have* had considerable experience. . . ."

One of the painful facts of life is that there are many speakers . . . but few good ones. Practice makes perfect in public speaking as in anything else—but it must be the right kind of practice. The wrong kind of practice merely strengthens a speaker's bad habits —like a week-end golfer grooving his errors by hitting practice shots without professional guidance.

Years of "practice" have enabled many executives to overcome their fear of speaking before groups of people. Unfortunately, they are not always aware that their skill as speakers hasn't kept pace with their confidence. Even their best friends hesitate to mention it.

The executive who is a skillful speaker has a tremendous advantage. The larger the group to which he is talking, the more obvious this advantage becomes. The skilled speaker:

— *commands greater interest and attention,*

> — *presents his ideas more clearly and persuasively,*
> — *establishes closer rapport with his audience,*
> — *projects a better image of himself and his company.*

There's no mystery to making a good talk. You can learn the principles and apply them just as well as anyone else. Not like a polished professional, perhaps, but certainly in a manner which will reflect credit on you and your company. After all, that's the main objective, isn't it? If you get to be too good, people will be dragging you away from home and fireside to talk to every group in the country.

The techniques described in this book are used by professional speakers everywhere. They are not illegal, unethical or patented. You can use them with the same honesty and pride with which you would try to copy a good golf swing. The executive who ignores them is turning his back on the accumulated knowledge and experience of some very talented people—speakers who achieve night after night, week after week, the very results he seeks.

Bishop Fulton J. Sheen was once asked how long it took him to prepare one of his thirty minute television talks. "Only a few hours," he replied.

The listener was amazed. "How do you do it?" he marveled.

"Well," said the Bishop, "you must remember, I've had 40 years' experience."

Even with 40 years experience, you might not be another Bishop Sheen. Yet just a few hours' thought and practice—following the correct principles—can make you a better speaker than you are. The more you practice, the more skillful you'll become.

WHAT MAKES A SPEECH GOOD OR BAD?

THE REASON SO MANY PEOPLE make poor speeches is that they've never stopped to analyze what a good speech really is.

A speech is the *oral* expression of a person's ideas or opinions. The important word in this definition is *oral*. It imparts certain advantages but also places distinct limitations on what even the finest speaker can hope to accomplish. It also dictates the methods and materials he should use.

A speech that reads well doesn't necessarily listen well. Words, phrases, and sentence structure that are familiar to the eye may be strange to the ear. Why? Because they don't sound the way we are accustomed to hearing people talk. That automatically makes them harder to understand.

A reader can stop and reflect for a minute any time he chooses to do so. If something wasn't completely clear, he can refer back and read it again. The listener has no such choice; he has to move ahead at the speaker's pace regardless of whether he wants to or not.

That's why a competent speaker takes such pains to make himself crystal clear. A good speech—like a good popular magazine article—consists of a surprisingly small number of ideas. Each, however, is securely related to the main theme; each is liberally illustrated and explained with stories, anecdotes and "for instances." The result is clarity, impact and enjoyable listening.

One of the big differences between the professional speaker and the amateur is that professionals never pile one abstract idea on top of another. Each concept is brought down to earth, clarified by anecdotes and illustrations, and firmly secured in the listener's mind before the speaker introduces another one.

One secret of an effective speech is simplicity. Most good speeches are organized around one fundamental idea. This central idea is the glue which holds a speech together in the mind of the listener. Everything else in the speech is related to it in some way—amplification, explanation, supporting reasons, proof, etc. The speaker who crossbreeds two ideas in one speech lessens the impact of both. After all, how much can you explain to a man, thoroughly and convincingly, solely by word of mouth, in the time at your disposal?

A good speech uses conversational language—it has more color, impact, and is more readily understood than the language many of us use in written communications. Think it over and you'll realize that the most effective speeches sound as though the speaker were talking *directly* to each person in the audience. Listen closely to his speech and you'll find he uses the familiar phraseology of face-to-face conversation.

He sounds, not like a textbook or an essay, but like a man talking directly to other men.

In appreciating the difference between a good speech and a poor one, it's important to realize that many messages which are presented in speech form never should be. They are too complicated, too involved, too closely reasoned for effective verbal presentation. They are much better presented in written form which people can read and study at length.

Consider the President's budget message to Congress, for example, or his annual report on the state of the economy. No speaker in the world could—in the time allotted—present so much information, so much reasoning, and so many abstract ideas in a form which would interest the average listener. The subject matter is so complicated that even the most alert and intelligent listener should study the text to fully comprehend the contents.

No matter how much skill and wisdom goes into the creation of these messages, they don't make good speeches. They are presented in speech form simply as part of the drama and protocol of government.

A great speech is a great *oral* message—it should be directed at listeners, not readers. People think of Lincoln's Gettysburg Address as a great speech. Actually, it left the audience cold and apathetic—most of those present completely missed the significance and import of what the Civil War President said. But Lincoln was concerned with more than his immediate audience—he was talking for the benefit of all mankind.

What Lincoln wrote was a great human message, a great *editorial*. But it was a message more powerful for the eye and the mind than for the ear. The ideas were too complicated, too abstract, to grasp at one listening. It wasn't until years later—long after the speech had appeared in print—that its meaning and import were fully understood and appreciated. Only then was it recognized as one of the classic messages of all history.

If you are writing for posterity, a speech to be *read* and *reread* down through the ages, don't worry about your listeners. But be sure the occasion warrants it. If the people you want to impress, the people you want to receive your message, are right there in the audience, don't try to give a Gettysburg Address. Use the techniques in this book. Design your talk to and for the people who are listening, and present it in the best possible way for a *listener* to understand and appreciate. Listeners—not readers—are a speaker's judge and jury.

CHOOSING A TOPIC

THE SUCCESS OF A SPEECH DEPENDS ON —

WHAT you say, and

HOW you say it.

Frequently, especially in your own business organization, a group of people may gather together for the specific purpose of listening to you speak on a certain matter. The topic is already settled.

Other times, you may be invited to address an outside organization on a subject of their choosing. Or the topic, in some instances, may be left up to you.

At this point we'd like to introduce a basic rule: DON'T SPEAK JUST FOR THE SAKE OF SPEAKING! No amount of words can make up for a lack of ideas. Don't agree to address any audience, anywhere, unless you have something to say, something you believe in, something you think would interest your listeners.

It's a rare person who can give a convincing talk on a topic he knows little about. And who wants to? Select the familiar—your work, your hobby, something you've studied or given considerable thought to. Make your selection meaningful—something you can get excited about, which moves you so you can move others. Then you will have that confidence on

15

the platform which is needed for success—the confidence of knowing what you're talking about.

If you're asked to talk on an unfamiliar subject, examine it carefully; some facet of it might strike a spark. If no glimmer can be found, suggest to the program chairman other topics which might fit the occasion and interest the audience. If you can't agree on a subject, then sit this one out. The smart speaker with nothing to say refrains from saying it.

It's common knowledge that this rule is often violated. It's one of the main reasons why there are many stuffy, unoriginal, insincere, uninspired public speeches.

How does it happen? A busy executive is invited to speak to a prestige-laden group on a topic of current interest. Despite the fact that he hasn't given the subject much thought, he's urged to accept. So—flattered and urged on—he agrees.

He doesn't have time to do the necessary research, so his public relations department and assorted ghost writers take over. The executive doesn't care too much for the manuscript they come up with, but what alternative does he have? He makes a few changes, practices a few times, then *reads* it before his distinguished audience.

When it's over, his colleagues rush to congratulate him, Nice job! Wonderful speech! But was it? Can a man really make a first-class impression reading someone else's words, someone else's thoughts, backed by nobody's convictions?

That same executive, if he had selected a familiar topic on which he had strong convictions, and presented those convictions in simple fashion backed by anecdotes from his own experience, had a golden opportunity to make a deep and lasting impression. Instead, he gave another run-of-the-mill talk.

Even when speaking on a subject with which you are familiar, it pays to do some research; gather more speech material than you need. Libraries, personal interviews, books, newspapers—all can enlarge your knowledge about your topic.

Study all sides of your subject. Audiences quickly detect and discredit one-sided viewpoints. Base your conclusions on a balanced consideration of all the evidence and issues, backed by quotes from noted authorities. This is not only a matter of integrity on the platform—it's the only sure way to convince your audience.

Well informed speakers keep reference files. Covering a wide range of selected topics, these can be organized in a card file or Manila folders and indexed for rapid access. Such a file builds up over a period of time with personal notes, stories, anecdotes, quotations, newspaper and magazine clippings. While not a substitute for original thinking, a reference file is invaluable in triggering the imagination, and as a source of facts and illustrations.

Like the student with straight A's on his report card, you will excel on the platform only if you've done your homework. And remember this observation of one successful speaker: "On an unknown topic, I always remain silent and run the risk of being thought a fool, rather than speak and remove all doubt."

ORGANIZING YOUR SPEECH

INDISPENSABLE AS IT IS, content alone won't insure a successful talk. The raw material which has been gathered to build the speech now needs to be organized.

Without organization, the speech will be like the talk given by an inexperienced speaker to a farmers' Grange in a Midwestern town. The speaker talked for two hours using every conceivable fact and illustration which applied to his theme.

After he was through, the president of the Grange shook his hand and said:

"You had lots to say and you came through real loud, but we like a man that *bales* his hay before he delivers it."

Different formulas for constructing a speech, each with its own advantages and drawbacks, can be found in any speech text. The three part outline— OPENING, BODY and CLOSING—is the simplest yet one of the most effective.

Following this outline, you can methodically organize your speech like a lumberjack felling an oak.

OPEN the talk with a swing of the axe at the right spot on the tree trunk. In the BODY of the speech, chop away until the oak is ready to topple. Finally, just before he shouts "timber," the lumberjack takes a last mighty swing. Similarly, CLOSE your talk with a strong remark which drives home the message.

One thing, perhaps, ought to be added to this formula even though it is not actually part of your speech—ACKNOWLEDGMENT OF THE INTRODUCTION. Sometimes this isn't necessary; other times it is very much in order! *BE READY*

A toastmaster once introduced a well known business figure. He told the audience the distinguished speaker they were about to hear had graduated from YALE and then took a half-hour to expand on each letter—Y stood for Youth, A for Aggressiveness, L for Love, and E for Enthusiasm.

Finally, with the audience near exhaustion, the speaker rose to give his talk. Wiping his brow, he began by turning to the toastmaster and saying,

"That was some introduction, but I'm sure everyone in this room is thankful I didn't go to the MASSACHUSETTS INSTITUTE OF TECHNOLOGY."

When you feel it's proper to acknowledge your introduction by the toastmaster, do so. But keep it *brief!* And don't ramble from the acknowledgment into your speech. Acknowledge the introduction, then STOP! Give the audience a moment to realize that something is about to happen. Then draw a bead and hit them right between the eyes with the opening sentence of your speech.

"Start With the Body"

In preparing your speech, start with the *BODY* first. Once you know what the animal looks like, it's much easier to add the head and tail.

To begin with, what's your central theme? In one sentence, what's the impression you are trying to make with this speech? What are the big "ideas" you would like to convey? Don't make a move until you've decided this question. Otherwise you may wind up with a speech that starts in all directions and goes nowhere.

Suppose, for example, you've opened a new plant in a town where your company has never operated before. The local Chamber of Commerce has invited you, the manager of a new enterprise in town, to address their weekly luncheon. What should you say?

Using good sense, you decide to keep it simple. You feel the important things to get across are that your company is glad to be located there, you appreciate the cooperation the town has given to date, and you plan to be a good neighbor in the future.

From that point on, the speech practically writes itself. You have your central theme—just go ahead and prove or demonstrate it.

Your company is glad to be there? Prove it by showing the care you took in choosing this location, describing some of the advantages. If certain aspects of your business are working out well because of the new location, tell about them.

You appreciate the cooperation you've received? Give some details—"for instances" giving credit to local authorities and others who lent a hand.

You expect to be a good neighbor? How? Why? Is your operation a clean, unobjectionable one? Do you have a record of stable employment and good labor relations? Are you a growing enterprise which will help the community? Mention these things too.

There—with little strain and effort—is the outline for a satisfactory talk. Not sensational, perhaps, but who expects sensationalism at a local Chamber of Commerce luncheon? The occasion calls for an informative, goodwill chat, and that's what you've delivered.

Having decided on a central theme, the BODY of your speech should be a succession of points which develop it. But *don't* present them as a deadly serious exercise in abstract logic. Lighten and brighten your talk by using the following narrative techniques. They are designed to make an audience sit up and be absorbed in what you're saying.

1. *Illustrate main points with concrete examples.* Don't speak more than a minute or two without a "for instance" which illustrates the point being made.

Note how a speaker giving a talk on CONCENTRATION gets his point across with this story:

"Jack Harris, a production manager, had to put together a presentation for his boss. Just as he started to jot down some notes, the phone rang about an overdue inventory report. He buzzed his secretary for the inventory file, and she also brought in the mail. Jack spotted a letter on top complaining about machine maintenance. He picked up the letter, read it, and started for the machine shop. As he passed the program office, a schedule chart caught his eye. He started to examine the chart but a supervisor interrupted him to sign a hiring request. That reminded Jack of another personnel problem. So he took the hiring request and headed for the employment office. On the way he passed the cafeteria. The coffee

21

smelled so tempting he decided it was time to interrupt his busy morning and have a coffee break.

"Does this kind of work schedule sound familiar? Unless there's a conscious effort to avoid it, most of us find ourselves hopping from one small job to another. We let the little things rob us of our bigness, let interruptions interrupt our interruptions. Doesn't this story suggest an obvious way that executive could have accomplished a great deal more? All he had to do was: *finish one job at a time.*"

Anecdotes, stories, analogies, will be remembered by an audience long after most of the speech is forgotten. Remembering the example, the listener recalls the idea it illustrated.

2. Use examples involving widely known individuals or incidents to further increase audience interest.

Even a reference to antiquity, such as the following illustration, can provide a striking parallel of a modern-day idea:

"The practice of DELEGATING responsibility is about as old as organized effort. When Moses was leading his people through the wilderness out of Egypt, he found himself under a staggering burden of management. Maybe that was one of the reasons it took him 40 years to find his way. It was his father-in-law, Jethro, who straightened him out. Jethro told him that he had to share his responsibilities with others.

"You'll find the whole story in Exodus. 'And Moses chose able men out of all Israel, and made them heads over the people, rulers of thousands, rulers of hundreds, rulers of fifties, and rulers of ten. And they judged the people at all seasons; the hard cases they brought unto Moses but every small matter they judged themselves'."*

3. *Express statistics and complex ideas in familiar terms.*

When you use statistics, "Rattle the Bones."

Except for those few listeners who may be technically trained, an audience usually has difficulty grasping the significance of quantitative data which is verbally presented. To make numbers mean something, present your statistics in everyday terms.

For example, the cost of sending the first astronaut to the moon is estimated at 20 billion dollars. This sum is so vast, it's hard for the typical listener to visualize. Suppose you divide the 20 billion dollars by the almost 200 million people in this country. That makes $100 for every man, woman, and child. Now the audience begins to get the picture. Or, how about taking the approximate 200,000 miles from the earth to the moon and working out a dramatic relationship to the 20 billion dollars? If a bridge of ten dollar bills, set end to end, were stretched from here to the moon, their sum would be about 20 billion dollars.**Impressive to an audience? You bet it is!

Even the simplest numerical relationships tend to confuse people. A speaker mentioned in his talk that the total snowfall during a typical winter in the city of Syracuse, New York, averages 120 inches. Little reaction was noted from the audience. In his next talk, the speaker made a simple conversion, stating

---

*By Dr. J. D. Cooper as published in the Philadelphia Inquirer.

**Example from speech given by R. J. Brown, General Electric Co. to Eastern Advertisers Association.

the snowfall averaged 10 feet. One listener summed up the general reaction, "Wow, that sure is a lot of snow!"

Complex ideas, like statistics, should also be brought down to earth and put in simple, understandable terms for the audience. If the ideas can be dramatized as well, their impact will be that much greater. In doing so the speaker must gauge his audience. There are degrees of simplification. The speaker must use discretion in drawing a fine balance between ease of comprehension on the one hand, and sufficient detail and depth on the other.

Remember Colonel Glenn's vivid press conference description of his first orbital flight? To illustrate that his flight was only a small first step, he held one hand over his head and asked the audience to imagine the diameter of the earth to be about 80 inches—only slightly more than his own height. If this were the case, he stated, his orbital flight had only taken him a little more than an inch above the surface. He concluded: "If you think of the enormity of space, it makes our efforts seem puny."

4. *A fourth technique is the "YOU" approach.*

As one sage put it:

"An egotist talks to you about himself, a gossip talks to you about others, and a good SPEAKER talks to you about yourself."

Audiences are groups of individuals with the same emotions and desires possessed by all of us. Therefore, beam your message at each person. Ask this question:

"How can I say this to directly affect each listener?"

Replacing each "I" in the talk with "You" or "We" helps. But the important consideration in keeping audience attention is to be concerned about what affects each listener. Thinking of other people's interests, you will automatically speak and act that way.

For example, don't just talk about "the confiscatory taxation system in this country." Instead, hit home with, "Thirty-five cents of every dollar *You* earn is taken as tax."

Opening Your Talk

Once you have the BODY of the talk, the next step is to find a good OPENING.

It would be nice if the audience would be sitting on the edges of their chairs waiting eagerly to hear what you have to say. But the fact is they won't be. Many speeches are dull, uninspired, boring. Why should they assume that the next one will be any different? The truth is that most of your listeners will be sitting back in their seats with a "show me" attitude.

Let's face it. They can't be blamed for not knowing what an interesting, dynamic, amusing speaker you are. You have to show them—and the best time is right now . . . immediately. Begin by saying or doing something which gets their attention, which promises that this talk will be interesting, amusing, informative.

If you have a flair for showmanship, use it. A Chicago audience, about to hear a talk on traffic accidents, was startled to see a coffin carried to the stage by six pallbearers. The coffin was set down by the microphone, the lid creaked opened, and the speaker rose to give his talk. He had the rapt attention of everyone in the room.

Too undignified for your taste? That's not an unusual reaction—but do you think the audience for one moment worried about the speaker's dignity? They admired his imagination and daring and were fascinated by the fact that here was a speaker who knew how to dramatize his ideas.

Still too rich for your blood? All right, you don't have to be carried on stage in a coffin. But you still should face the fact that a good speaker *must* be entertaining. Most people don't enjoy sitting and listening to dull words of wisdom, no matter how significant.

Look over your talk. What is the most interesting thing in it *from the audience's point of view?* Your whole talk should be designed to interest the audience, but what is the *most* interesting facet? Pull it out and build your opening around it. Then work out a transition from that opening into the body of your talk.

Does your speech have any sort of challenge for the audience—one to make them sit up and take notice? Why not use it for an opening?

What is the most interesting anecdote in your speech? Could you use it as a starter to open the subject?

Do you have an amusing story which is pertinent to the subject you are about to discuss? Seasoned speakers often start with a humorous story to get audience attention and put them in a good mood. But don't use a joke that isn't related directly to what you have to say, and don't tell it as if you expected a big laugh. Tell it to illustrate the point and then proceed calmly into your subject.

Whatever you do, resist the amateurish compulsion to apologize. Many speakers apologize before they even begin. They apologize for talking on this topic, for not being the expert they are billed as, for not being replaced by a better speaker. Sidestep the hand-wringing and make your opening a positive one.

If you desire to inject a note of humility in your opening remarks, do it subtly—with a dash of humor —as one clever speaker does whenever he addresses a body of experts:

"When I was asked to give this talk, I felt like the skeleton in the doctor's closet . . . I didn't have the guts to say no."

The Closing

It's vital to have a good closing.

It's also vital to know when to *use* it. How often have you heard a speaker ruin a good talk by not knowing when to stop? He reaches the end of his ideas, wonders if he really made his point, then proceeds to repeat himself. The audience squirms.

Ever watch the Kentucky Derby? The winner often won with a "garrison finish," named after the racing technique of jockey Snapper Garrison. Snapper's strategy was to save some of his horse's energy for the last turn . . . and then sprint to the wire in a surge of power.

From a timing standpoint, your last remarks are the most important part of the speech. End with a purpose—since the points you make in the "home stretch" are those the audience will remember most. This is the spot to drive home your point of view and persuade your audience to act on it.

If the objective of your talk is to urge the audience to do something, tell them specifically what you want them to do—now! Then sit down.

If you've been trying to prove something, restate your main points, state the conclusion, and sit down! But don't take more than thirty seconds to do it—don't start repeating the whole speech.

If there is a story which sums up what you've been talking about, tell it. Then sit down!

Knowing when to stop is an essential ingredient of any good speech. Few talks are spoiled by the speaker stopping too soon; thousands are ruined by stopping too late. Don't begin a talk without knowing exactly how you plan to end it. Then follow your plan!

DELIVERY

Your speech is prepared—

OPENING, BODY, CLOSING.

The question now is, how are you going to deliver it?

MEMORIZING a speech is a tricky business for most speakers. True, an experienced actor can memorize a script, and then deliver it with flawless diction— complete with gestures, vocal variety, and all the other niceties of good delivery. Any stage play is living testimony that words can be memorized and brought to life by skilled performers.

But few of us have this ability, and even for those who do this is making a speech the hard way. Memorizing a speech is tedious. Then, when giving the talk, the speaker is apt to concentrate so hard on remembering the next word or phrase that he falls easy prey to those platform bugaboos — memory lapses and mechanical delivery.

The speaker who sticks to a memorized text denies himself the flexibility to change pace in response to audience reaction. Also, lack of a spontaneous delivery further narrows the chances of putting his message across.

Memorizing a talk is possible, but its many pitfalls strongly caution against its use.

READING a speech also results in a stilted delivery unless done with rare skill. Audience contact suffers when the speaker is slavishly chained to a manuscript, even if he reads well.

A program chairman who sat through a boring evening listening to one speaker after another read his speech once remarked with vehemence,

"There are three kinds of people who read speeches:

"First, the honest ones who carefully pile each page in front of them as they read, letting the audience keep track of how much more there is;

"Then there are the mysterious ones who keep the audience in suspense by putting each page under the others in their hand; and lastly . . .

"The sneaky ones who stack each page in front of them—then as the audience sighs in relief at the end, horrify everybody by picking up the whole pile and reading off the other side."

It is usually so hard for a speaker to establish audience rapport by reading a speech, that this method should only be used when it's necessary to follow exact wording.

If you must read, have the speech typed in capital letters, double spaced; triple spaced between paragraphs, with wide margins. It will be easier to read. Also, make sure a lectern will be available; it's an added burden to read a speech with no stand to hold the text.

Above all, remember this secret of good eye contact when reading—look up often at the audience, *particularly during the last part of each sentence or paragraph.* Your ideas will then carry through with maximum impact.

But having spent the time, study and effort to create a good speech, why read it? Why choose the method of presentation which guarantees the poorest reception for your message?

The caveman who rose by the campfire to address his tribe had no written script. He stood on his feet and said what was on his mind. It's a safe bet he used conversational language too, because there was no other.

That's still the formula for the best way to make a speech—one man getting on his feet and telling others what he has on his mind. The President can't do it very often—especially when he speaks for the nation. He has to carefully choose every word. But *you* can and *you* should, whenever possible. The advantages far outweigh the danger of verbal lapses or possible mistakes in grammar or sentence structure. Your speech becomes one man talking to another; it's sincere, vital, human, happening right here and now. And it's couched, as it should be, in your own natural language.

As a member of an audience, which speaker makes the greater impression on you—one who reads his speech, or one who talks directly to you, following a well-planned outline, but phrasing his thoughts in everyday language?

Why do so many businessmen read their speeches? Usually because they're afraid not to. They simply don't have sufficient confidence in their ability to think on their feet and state their ideas effectively in front of an audience.

Their fears are exaggerated. Virtually anyone with ability to achieve executive status also has the ability to organize his ideas effectively and, with a few simple notes, present them simply and clearly. It's an important talent—in small meetings or large, and the closer you move to the top of an organization, the more important it becomes. The executive who fails to develop this ability is seriously handicapped.

Notes for this type of EXTEMPORANEOUS speaking should consist simply of a list of main ideas you intend to cover, in proper sequence, perhaps with a subhead or two under each. When the speaker has covered the first item, he merely glances at his notes and takes up the next one. His talk doesn't wander —it follows a logical, preplanned outline. The main ideas for a 15 minute talk will usually fit on a single 3 x 5 card.

How can you be sure you will express each idea effectively? By practice—by doing it in advance five, ten, or twenty times, if necessary, until you are certain you can find adequate words. The speaker who doesn't rehearse thoroughly is taking chances. He may wind up like the businessman whose wife asked: "How did your talk go over?"

"Which one," he retorted disgustedly, "the one I intended to give, the one I did give, or the one I gave so brilliantly to myself on the way home in the car?"

Even speakers of the stature of Sir Winston Churchill rehearse their speeches. One day, while Churchill was taking a bath, his valet heard his voice over the splashing of the water. Sticking his head in the door, the valet inquired, "Did you call, Sir?"

"No," Churchill replied, "I was just giving a speech to the House of Commons."

When practicing, don't try to memorize anything! Simply talk about each idea until you can express it clearly—regardless of whether you say it the same way each time. Don't even try to remember exactly how you said it. Just talk about it enough times—until you're positive you can make it clear, one way or another.

If you're having trouble with a certain idea, write it out. Work it over. Find the best way to say it. But don't try to *memorize* any one way. Then, on the platform, you won't be paralyzed by the fear of forgetting something. You'll have the list of ideas in your hand and you know you can talk about each. Don't worry about remembering those "choice phrases" and you'll find yourself automatically using many of them.

When you think you're about ready, get a tape recorder and talk your speech into it. Then sit back and listen. There will be spots that can be improved, things you'll want to change. Perhaps your wife or a friend might have suggestions. But once again—don't memorize the changes. Just rethink the section and retalk it a few times so the right language is ready when you need it.

Also, don't memorize gestures, vocal variety, or facial expressions—let these, too, appear spontaneously as you speak.

Extemporaneous speaking enables you to adjust to any situation arising on the platform. This ability to tune in on the exact wavelength of the audience, plus your natural delivery, is what will put your message across.

Your address may have a few rough spots, but they'll

be far outweighed by your spontaneous style. You'll be a speaker who knows his material and *whose main purpose is to convince his audience*. This is public speaking at its best.

When learning this technique, try it for brief talks at first. As your confidence develops, use it for more important occasions. It's the best way to make an excellent speech anywhere, anytime. Master it, and you'll never again want to read a speech.

YOUR PLATFORM PERSONALITY

IN THE DAYS OF THE ROMAN EMPIRE, Nero was having a circus in the Coliseum. A Christian was thrown to a hungry lion. The wild beast pounced on him as the spectators cheered. But the Christian quickly whispered something in the lion's ear and the beast backed away in horror.

After this happened several times, the Emperor sent a centurion to find out what magic spell could make ferocious lions cower in fear. After a few minutes the guard came running back and said,

"The Christian whispers in the lion's ear—'After dinner, you'll be required to say a few words.' "

All speakers are nervous. The acute phase is called

stagefright and comes in many disguises. The mouths of some speakers get so dry they can hardly talk. Others can't think clearly, their hands tremble, knees shake, voices crack.

Stagefright can take the starch out of the strongest individual; it's the biggest scarecrow frightening people away from the platform. Even executives accustomed to making important decisions get butterflies in their stomachs when called upon to speak to a group of people . . . whether they're willing to admit it or not.

The marketing manager of a leading corporation was pacing up and down in a room near an auditorium where he had to address a large group. A woman entered the room.

"Are you nervous before you make a speech?", she asked.

"No, I never get nervous," the executive replied.

"Then," demanded the woman, "What are you doing in the ladies room?"

Stagefright can be licked. As you gain experience and confidence, you will bring it under control as a sprinter controls and uses his nervous energy in a quarter-mile dash.

In the first place, don't take the occasion too seriously. Thousands of other men have made speeches in similar situations—good speeches, bad speeches, and very bad. Yours won't be the worst. So relax—enjoy the experience and do your best.

To overcome the mental block of stagefright, breathe deeply while still sitting in your chair, just before

arising to speak. This will fill your blood stream with oxygen. While speaking pause often, each time taking a gulp of air. If you're scared, just keep it to yourself and no one will know the difference.

Most speakers are deadly afraid of forgetting what they were going to say . . . and every now and then a mental blackout does occur. The best speaker occasionally finds himself at a loss for words, particularly if he's tired from losing sleep the night before.

If you suddenly forget your next idea, here's a simple trick to bale yourself out. Just repeat in different words the last point made. Rephrasing the last paragraph gives your subconscious mind time to pick up the thread of the speech and put your derailed thoughts on the right track again.

Depending on the individual, nervousness manifests itself a dozen different ways. Hands tremble? Empty your pockets except for two short pieces of wood. When speaking, put your hands in your pockets and grip the pieces of wood until you settle down.

Properly controlled, nervous energy is the valued servant of all able speakers. Don't try to eliminate your nervousness, but become its master. A speaker without a reservoir of nervous energy would be as lacking in vitality as a dead fish.

Be Enthusiastic

A speaker without adequate preparation is like a car with an empty gas tank. A speaker without enthusiasm is like a car without even an engine.

Enthusiasm is essential in delivering your talk. Even with other techniques lacking, enthusiasm will go a long way toward putting your message over.

Enthusiasm begins with a good night's sleep. Then the secret is to believe in your talk. If a speaker doesn't have faith in what he's saying, how can he expect to convince an audience?

Don't, however, make the same mistake as a new minister in a small town. Finding only three people at his first service, he went down to them and asked if they still wanted to hear the sermon. One old farmer thought about it a moment, then replied:

"Wal, if I had a wagon-load of hay and went out to feed a herd of cattle and only found three cows . . . I'd sure feed 'em."

"I guess you're right at that," said the minister. Taking the message to heart, he went back to the pulpit and for a solid hour delivered one of his most enthusiastic sermons. He put all he had into it.

After the sermon was over, the minister. wiping his brow, went down to the farmer,

"Well, what did you think of it?"

The farmer raised one eyebrow,

"Wal, if I had a wagon-load of hay and went out to feed a herd of cattle and only found three cows . . . I sure as heck wouldn't give 'em the whole load."

Be sure your enthusiasm fits the audience. For a small audience an informal, subdued enthusiasm is most appropriate. It's not necessary to have an emotional outburst; your enthusiasm can show even if you whisper. As the audience builds up, more punch, force, and vitality are required.

Be Sincere

An ounce of sincerity is worth a pound of eloquence.

Sincerity, reflecting a speaker's personality, is indispensable on the platform. A pretentious speaker, lacking honesty and conviction, quickly loses the trust of his audience.

Be earnest and be YOURSELF. Unlike an actor portraying a fictitious character, you will achieve best results by projecting your own personality. Canned speeches, lacking sincerity, have little persuasive appeal.

Don't imitate other speakers. Develop YOUR own style—tailored to YOUR personality—emphasizing YOUR strong points. Then you will become a powerful platform personality in your own right, not just a carbon copy of someone else.

When Bill O'Dwyer was campaigning for Mayor of New York City, he would start his speeches with a sheet of paper in his hand. Looking around, he'd greet some of the people in the audience:

"Hi, Joe," "Hello, Bob," "Nice seeing you, Jack."

Then he would say, "I had no idea so many of my friends would be here tonight. I don't need any notes to talk to you people." With that, he would pitch away his paper and give the speech in his own natural, conversational manner . . . the audience loved him for it.

A newspaper reporter who had watched him do this at several meetings picked up the paper after one of the speeches. It was an old laundry bill.

A strong speaker never appears meek. Yet, he instills his authoritative remarks with humility . . . free from pride and arrogance.

41

The effective speaker doesn't talk down to his audience. No speaker can give a decent speech unless he respects the intelligence of his hearers. While temporarily captive, listeners should be treated with dignity, and not with a patronizing attitude. They will then be receptive to your ideas and your speech will be on its way to success.

Be EARNEST, be SINCERE, be HUMBLE. Above all, be YOURSELF.

PLATFORM TECHNIQUE

A COMMON FAULT of the beginning speaker is to look down at the ground, up at the ceiling, out the window, at the lectern—everywhere except at the audience. Look at your audience! The communication process between speaker and listener demands direct audience contact. Except for quick referral to notes, look at your listeners—as if you were talking face-to-face to each person.

One simple technique is to consider the room in which you are speaking a billiard table. Shift at random to different parts of the table like a billiard ball, stopping at each point for about ten seconds, looking directly into an individual's eyes as you speak. This maintains close audience contact. Each person will feel you are talking directly to him.

In using the billiard table technique, don't swing back and forth like a pendulum on a grandfather clock. Too regular a movement will defeat your purpose by distracting the audience.

Remember the battle-cry of the American Revolution:

"Don't fire until you see the whites of their eyes."

When addressing a group of people, don't speak until you see the whites of *their* eyes.

Appeal to the Heart

People tend to like people who like them. Be friendly, show the audience you like them, and they will like you as a speaker.

Even a smile creates a bond between speaker and hearer. Show your good nature by maintaining a pleasant expression throughout the talk, smiling when appropriate—certainly when arising to speak. Stated another way, avoid frowning—this projects an unfriendly mood.

Some people have a hard time smiling even when they want to. George Kaufman, the famous playwright, was once described: "He always looks angry; inside he's happy, but his face hasn't heard the news." If you stop and think about it, twice as many muscles are needed to scowl as to smile. So why tire yourself out?

Remember, your purpose is to convince your listeners. Their receptiveness depends not only on the logic of what they hear, but whether they like you. You might be able to persuade them by sheer logic, but it will be a lot easier if you also have their good will. An audience is a bundle of emotional prejudices; the understanding speaker short circuits these prejudices with a friendly, reasonable attitude.

One moving emotional appeal sometimes outweighs a half-hour of factual argument. The effective speaker knows how to play on the heart strings of his hearers; to calm or excite their emotions as the case may be. F.D.R. rallied the nation with his plea that the only thing we had to fear was fear itself; Churchill bolstered England in its darkest hour with his appeal to blood, toil, tears, and sweat.

Emotional content is particularly effective at the conclusion of a speech; let your parting words inspire your listeners.

To sway your audience, appeal to the heart as well as the head.

Humor—A Sugar–Coated Pill

A serious talk delivered in a light vein is like a vitamin pill coated with candy—it has therapeutic value yet is pleasant to take.

Humorous anecdotes should be bona fide illustrations of the main points of a speech—never dragged in clumsily just to tell a story. Then, if the audience doesn't laugh at the mirthful aspects, the speaker won't be out in left field with a flat joke, embarrassed silence, and no easy transition back to the talk.

Skillfully used, humor is an asset, particularly in after-dinner talks; poorly used, it detracts. Laughter is music to a speaker's ears, but a humorous anecdote greeted with stony silence can be demoralizing—*unless it also stands by itself as a good illustration.*

For example, consider the following story. It was told by a speaker to show that no matter how important a man thinks he is, there's always someone else with an even bigger bump of conceit.

"Near the end of World War II, at the Yalta conference, the big three—Prime Minister Churchill, Premier Josef Stalin, and President Franklin D. Roosevelt—were having a little informal talk after one of the formal meetings.

Churchill lit a long cigar, puffed contentedly, and said,

"History will show that I, more than any other man, have shaped the destiny of mankind for the first half of this century."

Joe Stalin, lighting his big black pipe, responded, "NYET, God Almighty Himself has told me, Josef Stalin, that I have been chosen to rule the world."

F.D.R. looked across the table at Stalin and indignantly replied,

"Now, Joe, I never told you any such thing."

Usually a sure laugh-getter, this story would stand by itself even if it didn't strike an audience as being uproarious.

It's particularly important to rehearse anecdotes and memorize their punch lines. Timing is critical and the telling of a humorous story is as important as its content. Try your stories beforehand on friends to see if they really go over.

On a program with other speakers? Be sure to listen to the speakers who precede you. By coincidence, they may use your favorite anecdote. If so, better

46

find another story—or skip it entirely—when your turn comes. The same anecdote won't be funny the second time around.

Humor should be used sparingly with small audiences. Laughter is contagious; a story which just amuses 25 people may be uproarious to 100 or more.

The rule—use more humor for larger audiences.

Don't tell off-color stories. They may be a riot with the poker playing crowd, but usually tarnish a speaker's image in the eyes of his audience.

Use of humor should be tempered with judgment, depending on the occasion. Many a speech has been ruined because the speaker tried to be a comedian. On the other hand, an audience soon tires of a speech that is as serious as a belt line. On the platform, be neither a jester nor an undertaker.

Poise and Empathy

Strive for control.

When walking to the platform, watch for common mishaps such as tripping over the microphone cord. If interrupted during the talk by a loud speaker announcement, people entering or leaving, unnecessary noise, don't become flustered—calmly pause till the interruption is over, then proceed with your speech.

Listeners feel the same emotions as the speaker.

Actors are aware of this. In the theatrical field, it's called empathy. A flustered speaker flusters his audience. On the other hand, if you're poised, relaxed, and in control, then the audience will relax and be in the most receptive mood.

Just as an audience feels empathy with you as a speaker, you must be sensitive to their reaction. A mechanical transcription can't deviate from what has been recorded, but you have the flexibility to shift direction in accord with audience response.

Many an insensitive speaker, like a truck horse with blinders, won't take one step from his planned talk even though most of the audience has either walked out or fallen asleep. At the first sign of audience restlessness, the discerning speaker changes pace or shortens his talk. Listeners have no way of knowing the speech has been modified or cut.

Conversely, if you have their rapt attention and they're thoroughly enjoying themselves, you might add *cautiously* to what you planned to say. Inject off-the-cuff remarks. If not overdone, ad-libbing can be one of the joys of speech making.

Speak to an audience as you would have them speak to you.

CONTROLLING YOUR VOICE

FOR BETTER OR WORSE, your voice reveals you. Listeners form an immediate impression of you from how you sound—friendly or cold, honest or false, strong or weak. This impression is unscientific; listeners would be hard pressed to explain why they like the sound of one man's voice and distrust another's.

The elements which blend together to produce the human voice are well known . . . and fortunately, easy to improve. A person can improve "how he says it" by working on four factors: Volume, Rate, Pauses, and Inflection.

Volume

Anyone can produce at least three levels of volume—low, normal conversation, and loud. This is the easiest way to achieve vocal variety. Experienced speakers obtain five or six levels, from a stage whisper to a shout.

Volume variation should be keyed to content. Ideas needing emphasis require considerable volume. On the other hand, somber points usually call for a low delivery. Between a shout and a whisper, you can use many variations of loudness to accent your words.

Put extra oomph into your opening and closing; an easy way to insure this is to direct those particular remarks to the listeners in the last row.

Rate

A baseball pitcher forces the batter to stay on his toes by changing pace. Do the same to your audience. Varying the SPEED at which you speak prevents monotony, keeps your listeners alert.

Important ideas should be delivered in deliberate stepping-stone fashion so they may sink in and be considered.

Transitional material can be delivered at a more conversational rate since not as much reflection is demanded from the audience.

A fast pace imparts urgency to what you're saying. Listen to Walter Winchell's or Drew Pearson's rapid-fire presentation. It gives their remarks vitality and a sense of urgent importance.

Pauses

Punctuate your speech with pauses to let your ideas sink in.

For greatest impact, pause a few moments after each important point. Let the audience chew over and digest what's been said. Don't lower your eyes during the pause; continue to look at the audience or contact will be broken. Some speakers even time the length of each pause by counting to themselves up to five.

Remember the Coca-Cola ads—THE PAUSE THAT REFRESHES. Each five second pause on the platform will also provide a welcome breather for you to refresh your thoughts before sailing off on a new tack.

Inflection

Franklin D. Roosevelt was a master of vocal inflection. It gave warmth and vibrance to everything he said, playing a large part in his election to four successive terms in the White House.

Inflection is the change in intonation and pitch which lends shades of meaning to what is said. While difficult to master, a great deal of understanding can be added by vocal inflection.

As a simple example of inflection—when a question is asked, a certain upward inflection is used. The same words, with a different inflection, could be used to indicate a statement of fact.

Vocal variety calls for harmonious blending of *VOLUME* variation, changes in the *RATE* of speaking, ample *PAUSES*, and skillful use of vocal *INFLECTION*. This is how a pleasing, colorful delivery is achieved.

At first, conscious effort will be required to master these techniques. As you gain experience, their use becomes largely subconscious. Your voice will automatically respond to the demands of each situation.

Deepen Your Voice

Some individuals, such as General Douglas MacArthur and former presidential candidate Thomas Dewey, have naturally deep, resonant voices, ideal for public speaking.

A person's voice generally increases in pitch under

51

stress or excitement. Most voices also sound higher pitched when talking louder. As speaking experience is gained, however, nervousness decreases and vocal tone drops.

Legend tells us that Demosthenes developed his speaking voice by going each day to the seashore and speaking over the roar of the breaking waves with his mouth full of pebbles. Nowadays, thin voices can be deepened through diaphragmatic breathing exercises. Vocal or singing lessons will work wonders with the tonal quality of most voices. The superior voice is usually the better-trained voice.

Congressman Brooks Hays of Arkansas once described how he was taught vocal projection in a public speaking course in college.

"At the beginning of the course, each student was given a mouthful of marbles. After each practice speech, we were allowed to reduce the number by one marble. After we lost all our marbles, we became accomplished public speakers."

STAGING YOUR TALK

DRESS AND MANNER are important in creating an impressive platform image. Dress conservatively; you don't want the audience distracted from your remarks by unconventional clothes. Stand tall—a speaker who slouches tends to give the impression that he is also sloppy in his thinking. A snappy, on-the-toes appearance stamps you as an alert individual.

Don't be concerned about minor details such as putting your hands in your pockets. It's far more important to act natural than worry about small infractions. It is wise, however, to empty pockets of keys and coins. While the speaker may be unaware he is jingling coins in his pockets, the sounds have considerable carrying power.

Be careful in using those slant faced stands called lecterns, employed for holding notes. They come in assorted shapes and sizes and are usually designed for the taller sex. Women, in particular, must be wary of using lecterns which may almost completely hide them. The shrewd speaker is never trapped in the ludicrous position of having just the top of his head visible to the audience.

During the talk, don't drape yourself over the lectern or grasp it with the death clutch of a drowning man. Also, don't refer too often to notes on the lectern.

If you don't have many notes, why not dispense entirely with the lectern? Most speakers only use it as a crutch. It's not really needed; without it you can increase audience contact by a giant step.

Gestures Help

Gestures fit action to words.

Gestures are difficult to learn; most speakers just

won't or can't let themselves go before an audience. Properly employed, however, gestures which emphasize, describe, and clarify the spoken word are among the hallmarks of a polished speaker.

During a recent election campaign, a cleaning woman picked up a discarded text after a political speech. In the margins were notes such as "Pause," "Take off glasses," "Wipe brow." Opposite one long paragraph, in capital red letters, was:

"ARGUMENT WEAK HERE. SHOUT AND WAVE YOUR ARMS."

Gestures that camouflage don't belong in any speech, but meaningful gestures can be a powerful tool. Channel your nervous energy into constructive paths by gesturing with your hands, arms, and even your body. This is the sensible solution to that familiar problem: What should a speaker do with his hands?

There is virtually no limit to the different types of gestures which may be used. With such an endless variety, be sure not to overwork any particular gesture which may be your favorite. Reject with a push of the hands away from you, caution with an open palm, point with the index finger, divide in two with a vertical movement of the hand—these are only a few of the many variations available.

For creative gesturing, answer this question, "How can this idea be physically described to the audience?"

Use gestures as a surgeon uses his scalpels—vital at the proper moment, but never used just because they're available.

Consider Audience Size

Many a speaker has delivered a talk to a large audience that was a sensational success, then fallen into the trap of delivering the same talk, in the same way, to a small audience—and had the talk go over like a lead balloon.

In thinking about the effect of audience size, first examine the unlikely case of a speaker talking to an audience of *one* person. This can't be more than one-way conversation. A speaker would be artificial if he read his talk, followed copious notes, or used a microphone. In person-to-person discussion, few gestures and normal volume are appropriate.

Now boost the audience to twenty-five people. Your talk should still be informal, at conversational speed, with few notes. A microphone is not required. Even a lectern might impose an obstacle between you and your listeners. Furthermore, the room will probably be small; the perceptive speaker will not project himself too strongly. A speech to a small group should be relaxed for maximum audience contact.

But let's swing up to an audience of one hundred. You now need more vigor in your remarks. Humor begins to have more impact. You should deliver the talk more slowly and with more force since the larger room will absorb vocal energy. In short, audience size dictates that your talk become less of a conversation and more of a speech.

Now let's take a big jump to an audience of three hundred or more. Speaking to this many people requires considerable force, slower paced delivery, and a full range of gestures. This audience will respond to even slightly humorous comments. Notes and lectern can be used without distracting the listeners, most of whom will be seated some distance from the platform.

The perils in transition from a small to a large audience were strikingly demonstrated during a recent speech contest run by a large corporation. The company ran ten speech classes concurrently, each class consisting of 20 employees. At the conclusion of the 16-week course, each class selected one student to compete in a graduation speech contest. All 200 students were now in the audience. Each speaker, accustomed to talking to his own smaller class of 20 students, spoke so softly he could hardly be heard. To a man, they failed to realize that the larger audience, in a larger room, required greater force and volume.

Television sometimes presents a contrast between speaking styles for large and small audiences. Many times a speaker, talking directly to a large studio audience, simultaneously appears, via the small screen, in the intimacy of living rooms across the nation.

The speaker naturally delivers his speech in a style consistent with his large audience. But to the TV viewer, he may appear to be overdoing it, since the TV screen brings the speaker into the closeness of a small room with only a few people listening. Here the speaker is really on the horns of a dilemma brought about by modern technology.

Microphones Are Tricky

Use of a microphone also depends on audience size. With larger audiences a microphone should be used to amplify your voice.

Sensitivity of different microphones varies widely. Acoustical pickup depends on the distance of the speaker's lips from the microphone; the proper distance should be determined and the microphone positioned beforehand for best results. Also, the mike should be checked out to make sure it is working properly.

In using the mike, talk slightly louder than conversational level. Prevent fading by speaking at all times directly into the microphone. Avoid excess movement on the platform; each time you turn away from the microphone your words will be lost to the audience (unless you use a lapel mike or one fastened around your neck).

When raising your voice, step back a bit from the microphone or it will over-amplify. When whispering, step into the mike for subtle vocal shadings. As with the lectern, don't drape yourself over the mike, or hold on to it for support.

A microphone can be a powerful device when speaking to larger audiences; but like any precision instrument, use it with care and skill.

Props—A New Dimension

A picture is worth a thousand words (even though it still takes words to express that idea).

The inventive speaker uses props and visual aids to convey his message through a listener's eyes. Audience comprehension jumps through use of more than one sense—sight as well as sound. This is particularly true of business and technical presentations which lean heavily on statistical and technical data.

Charts, slides, models, exhibits, should supple-

ment but never completely take the place of a talk. Visual aids should be simple, understandable, and LARGE ENOUGH TO BE SEEN BY THE AUDIENCE. Limited only by imagination, they are another valuable addition to your speaker's tool kit.

Planning to use a blackboard, easel, slide projector, screen? Make sure they're set up for use beforehand. Otherwise you might spend the first fifteen minutes of your talk making mechanical arrangements while the audience sits and stews.

Some don'ts:

> *Don't* expose your prop or visual aid until you're ready to discuss it.

> *Don't* turn your back on your listeners—talk to the audience, not the prop.

> *Don't* hide a visual aid by standing in front of it.

> *Don't* have written material passed out while you're speaking. The audience will read the material and be diverted from what you're saying; distribute written material and other handouts after you've finished.

Props can dramatize your speech . . . if used correctly. If the props are poorly handled, the entire presentation suffers. Practice using your props when you're practicing your talk . . . don't be taken unawares like the candidate at a political rally. He was told by an exuberant program chairman that a cannon would go off as he rose to give his speech.

The program chairman requested: "Would you please begin your speech by saying—HARK, I HEAR THE CANNONS ROAR." The speaker readily agreed, and repeated the phrase to himself a few times.

Finally his time came on the program. The speaker was introduced and rose to give his talk, completely forgetting the cannon. It went off behind him with a thunderous roar:

— B O O M —

Startled, he blurted into the microphone,

"What the hell was that?"

Rehearse ahead of time with your props until you can handle them as skillfully as a magician pulling rabbits out of a hat; they'll add a new dimension to your talks.

Time Is Critical

A minister once remarked, "In giving a sermon, no souls are saved after the first half-hour."

The same rule can be applied to a speech. Yet speakers who drone on endlessly are common occurrences.

Find out from the program chairman how much time will be available for your talk. In practice sessions, and when actually giving the talk, fit your message to that time—neither too brief nor too long. The intelligent speaker doesn't saturate his audience; he ends his speech while they still want to hear a bit more.

Even when no time is specified, an experienced speaker develops a sixth sense for how long he should speak to any particular audience.

When Adlai Stevenson was running for President, he was asked where he got his coat of tan.

"You've been playing golf," a woman accused him.

"No, I got sunburned making outdoor speeches in Florida," Stevenson replied.

"Well," said the woman, "If you got that brown, you talked too long."

After-dinner talks generally run 30 to 45 minutes. Luncheon talks should be less than a half-hour since people have to return to their offices. Length of presentations at professional society meetings are usually specified by the program committee, running anywhere from 10 to 45 minutes. An evening slide presentation, such as a travelogue, might run for an hour or more since the audience won't be working as hard as when listening to a speech.

In any case, use common sense in deciding how long to speak. The proper length of a speech can't be determined by a stop watch; it depends on the time required to put across your ideas . . . no more and no less.

It also depends on how long the audience enjoys listening. If people get restless and start looking at their watches, immediately shift into your closing remarks. Save the rest for another time. Don't wait till the audience starts shaking their watches to see if they've stopped running.

Follow that age-old speaker's motto:

"Stand UP, Speak UP, and Shut UP."

SPECIAL SITUATIONS —
INTRODUCING A SPEAKER

"My sympathies lies with the speaker
Whose knees grow suddenly weaker
As the toastmaster's lengthy patter
Turns out to be the speaker's subject matter."

When introducing a speaker, you must provide the binding that holds a program together without committing those cardinal sins: taking too much time, or stealing the speaker's thunder. The speaker is the main course; as toastmaster, you are at best only the appetizer.

Anyone making an introduction has an obligation to the speaker—to present him in the best light to the audience and make him feel welcome. The spotlight belongs on the speaker; the toastmaster should not divert its beam to himself.

The toastmaster introducing a number of individuals on a program has to know a little about each of their subjects. In a sense, his job is to give the audience a taste of everything on the menu but never a complete dinner.

One toastmaster explained it this way:

"I'm like the gateman at a bull fight; I open the gates

to let the bull in and out."

Your job as toastmaster is to draw speaker and listener together so they can communicate. This calls for warming up the audience somewhat in the manner of the comedian who gets the audience laughing just before the TV quiz show goes on the air.

After a speaker has finished, comment favorably on his talk—on something noteworthy he said, quote some of his own words, or praise his delivery. Then skillfully span the gap between that speech and the next part of the program.

In supplying a bridge from speaker to audience, you should sense and provide an emotional balance. After a serious speech creating a somber mood, inject a light touch . . . a sparkle bringing the audience to life again. On the other hand, if someone's comments have evoked gales of laughter, then supply a more serious overtone.

Specifically, how should you introduce a speaker? You know the speaker's name, background, and topic. What next?

There are several excellent formulas for introducing speakers. One of the best is the Borden formula* which consists of answering key questions.

1. WHY THIS SUBJECT?
2. Why this subject BEFORE THIS AUDIENCE?
3. Why this subject before this audience BY THIS SPEAKER?

Answer these three questions for each speaker in three minutes or less and you will have done a cred-

---

*"Public Speaking As Listeners Like It" by Richard C. Borden (Harper & Brothers, N. Y.)

itable job of introduction. All three questions don't have to be answered in the same sequence for each occasion, nor does each question have to be given equal time. Use them only as a guide.

Two essential points, however, belong in every introduction. One is the topic of the speech; the second is the name of the speaker.

A speaker invariably rises when he hears his own name; it's his cue that the introduction is ended and he should begin. Therefore, give the speaker's name only once, at the tail end of your introduction. This precludes the embarrassment, which often happens, of the speaker rising to speak before you've finished introducing him.

Pronounce his name distinctly and loudly enough to be heard by everyone — fight the overwhelming temptation to turn your head from audience to speaker until you've done so, then turn with a smile. Remain standing until the speaker takes his place to speak, then sit down—another introduction has been successfully concluded.

A simple aid to help you organize your introduction is to type the three key questions on a 3 x 5 inch white index card. Include spaces for the topic and speaker's name.

TOPIC	
WHY THIS SUBJECT	
BEFORE THIS AUDIENCE	
BY THIS SPEAKER	
SPEAKER'S NAME	

With a few of these cards handy in your wallet, it's simple to jot down notes under each question. And the essentials—speech topic and speaker's name—are in front of you to thwart any lapse of memory on the platform.

One last reminder: KEEP IT BRIEF!

THE IMPROMPTU TALK

OCCASIONALLY, you may be asked to say a few words without prior notice and without opportunity for adequate preparation. As former British Prime Minister Disraeli once observed: "Impromptu talks on the spur of the moment are difficult since the moment often arises without the spur."

The rule in that case is simple: if you have nothing to say, don't say it. The fact that you have been called upon carries no obligation to stand and make a brilliant speech. You are given an opportunity to speak if you want to. If you don't want to, the best policy is to politely and good-naturedly decline.

There are a hundred ways to decline gracefully. One man, for example, did it as follows: "In my position it is sometimes important that I should not say foolish things. It very often happens that the only way to help it is to say nothing at all. Believing that this is my present condition this evening, I must beg of you to excuse me from addressing you further." (Abraham Lincoln to the crowd of well-wishers who called on him in Gettysburg the evening before his Gettysburg Address.)

When should you accept? Only when there is something you really wish to say—then say it!

The man who is apt to be called upon for impromptu remarks is seldom taken completely unawares. If you think you might be asked to comment, listen carefully to the proceedings. Is there anything that strikes a responsive note — anything so important you would like to endorse the sentiment—anything you feel needs a note of caution?

When you are invited, get up and talk about that specific item. Then sit down. Don't ramble all over the waterfront. One good incisive comment—delivered in two minutes or less—can make an excellent impression; ten minutes of rambling definitely won't. In fact, a speaker who has a reputation for rambling probably won't be called on in the first place.

As in any good speech, an impromptu talk should reflect sincerely felt opinions and convictions. In the House of Commons, Disraeli once made a brilliant speech on the spur of the moment. That evening an admirer said to him:

"I was entranced by your impromptu talk. It's been on my mind all day."

"Madam," confessed Disraeli, "that impromptu talk has been on *my* mind for 15 years."

A CONFERENCE PRESENTATION

THE BUSINESS PRESENTATION to a deliberative group (usually less than a dozen people) sitting around a conference table is the dominant form of communication in industry today. When making such a presentation the spotlight is on *you*, with a select audience that really counts. Your career is at stake to an extent not found in any other speech situation.

The conference table affords direct confrontation with upper management. Here you face the men who will decide not only the matter you are presenting to them, but ultimately your future. An impressive ten minute presentation in that environment could have considerable impact in any profession. It's one of the routes to higher responsibility.

All the foregoing lessons in this book apply to the conference presentation, just as they apply to any talk before a small group. In addition, this type of business presentation has two salient features:

- high INFORMATION content, and
- heavy dependence on VISUAL AIDS

Communicate Information

Your primary purpose in making a business presentation should be to communicate information. Conferences are called to hear about and discuss the hard facts of business life—sales up 20% from last year, personnel turnover suddenly a problem, district warehouses again running low on inventory, the union now demanding eight instead of six paid holidays per year. Your listeners demand a factual presentation of the business situation.

The most common type of conference presentation is problem analysis—a business problem has arisen requiring management to take remedial action. Your job—to present the problem, analyze it, and recommend a solution. You can best accomplish this with a simple and direct organizational format:

a. Statement of PROBLEM
b. ANALYSIS of key elements, including assumptions and pertinent evidence
c. Alternate SOLUTIONS (with pros and cons of each)
d. Recommended ACTION plan

Don't become solution-minded too quickly. You wouldn't think much of a doctor who recommended an operation before thoroughly examining an ailing patient. Similarly, don't recommend a solution until you have presented a thorough analysis of the problem.

Consider alternate solutions. This indicates careful study on your part and allows conference participants to attack the problem from all angles. Make your presentation a balanced one by presenting the pros and cons of each alternative.

The problem will be on its way to resolution only after a decision is made to take action; therefore, be

70

sure to recommend one. This is the payoff; a specific recommendation for decisive action.

There are, of course, many other types of business presentations and briefings—the status report, the training program, the sales talk. The organization of each should be tailored to the message, with one common denominator—*high INFORMATION content.*

The Eyes Have It

The visual aid has come into its own in the conference presentation. It runs the gamut from grease-pencilled flip charts to multi-colored projection slides and movies. The spoken word plus pictures equals a presentation with maximum audience comprehension.

Avoid the common error of trying to design the visual aids before your talk has been prepared. That puts the cart before the horse. First figure out what you're going to say . . . then illustrate it.

The simplest form of visual aid (after the blackboard) is a crayon-pencilled outline of major points on flip charts. A set of flip charts is nothing more than a large pad of white paper (30″ x 40″) hanging from a portable easel. Keep the outline cryptic; then elaborate on each point in the outline when giving your presentation. Quick to prepare and easy to use, flip charts are also widely employed for presenting statistical data and sketches.

A number of companies are making increased use of projectors which employ standard letter-size charts or text (8½ x 11) as the basic visual aid. With a suitable projector, these sheets can be thrown on a wall or screen without darkening the room. These visual aids have the added advantage of being an easily reproduced size and format if letter-size copies are desired for distribution.

Use of slides is somewhat more complex, in their design, and in their presentation which requires a projector, screen, and darkened room. Slides are generally advisable for larger audiences, or for a highly polished presentation.

There are many other types of visual aids—flannel boards, film strips, moving pictures, live demonstrations. In choosing the best technique to illustrate the message, you must, like a tennis player, tailor your stroke to the occasion.

The most important thing to remember in *designing* visual aids is to keep them simple and pertinent. Use them because they serve a purpose, never for their own sake.

The most important thing to remember in *using* visual aids is that they are aids; don't expect them to make the entire presentation for you.

Conference Psychology

Recognize and learn to deal with the powerful psychological factors that will be at work on each individual who is sitting around the conference table. The collective judgment of the participants has been gathered to bear on the problem at hand. Therefore, either during or after your presentation, be prepared for discussion from the floor—questions, comments, criticisms.

Some participants will feel compelled to talk at great length and will not consider the conference a success unless they dominate the discussion. Others will freeze in the presence of their superiors; many of their good ideas will be bottled up in their transmission system.

One school of thought has it that the average participant in a business conference is a poor listener. Instead of concentrating on what others are saying, he is only concerned with what he wants to say. When he does listen, he is more influenced by who is talking rather that what is being said. He is not open-minded; everything he does hear is filtered through a built-in screen of organizational prejudices and jealousies.

That may be an over-statement, but one vital element in conducting a conference is to get the participants focused on the problem and its solution, rather than on themselves.

Men in a conference don't like to be preached to. They want to discuss things, to show their colleagues how bright they are, and to project their own interests. Therefore, make your presentation brief and give everyone a chance to talk.

If each conferee shares in the decisions reached, they will feel in partnership with you. If necessary, ask leading questions to encourage discussion of your presentation. When fielding a question which doesn't have a black and white answer, stimulate discussion by reversing the tables and asking the questioner for *his* views on the matter. Just make sure the discussion doesn't wander too far afield.

One way to keep the conference on track is to ask one of the participants to serve as a Reminder.* This

---

*Irving J. Lee, "How to Talk with People" p. 162, Harper & Bros. New York.

can be done either with or without the knowledge of the other participants. The Reminder's sole job is to help keep the conference focused on the problem. Every time the discussion veers into a side road he tactfully steers it back to Main Street, through such techniques as re-phrasing the central issue and making frequent summaries.

When asked a question, don't jump to answer. Everyone likes to think his questions are incisive and penetrate to the heart of the matter; if you reply too quickly, the questioner may feel you thought his question shallow. Therefore, stop a moment, and give some thought to the query.

Assuming the question is sensible, you might comment:

"That's a good question, Jack"
or

"Bob, you've put your finger on one of the key issues."

The vest buttons of the questioner will pop off at that point and he will be on your side for the remainder of the conference.

When responding to a critical question or comment, always mention the name of the questioner. There is no sound as sweet to a man as his own name. It will go a long way toward disarming the most antagonistic critic.

A successful conference with a group reaching consensus rarely happens by accident. It comes about because you have acquired the skill to make an effective business presentation. It comes about because a climate has been created in which men talk and listen reasonably to each other. It comes about because you have conducted the conference in a manner that welds together the best ideas from each participant. Those are the highlights of a successful conference —use them the next time you have to make a presentation in that panelled room with a long oval table. Who knows, it might be where you win *your* next big promotion.

THE AFTER-DINNER TALK

IT'S A FACT OF LIFE that after-dinner speaking is monopolized by men . . . women can't wait that long. Seasoned speakers also agree that while after-dinner speaking appears to be the easiest kind of speech to give, in reality no other speech situation is as taxing on the speaker.

The situation is a familiar one, repeated thousands of times each week, with no end in sight. The audience has enjoyed a late cocktail hour, then dined on the usual banquet fare of fried chicken and green peas. After dinner, the toastmaster spends a tedious hour introducing a long string of local dignitaries at the head table, interspersing his remarks with forced bits of humor.

He now turns to you. In his own inimitable fashion,

he builds you up as a dynamic speaker, an expert from afar—carrying an inspiring message guaranteed to not only make the audience *laugh*, but also make them *think*.

Your job is a simple one—just live up to that introduction. Looking at the well-fed, and by now drowsy audience, you wonder if you can even get them to listen, much less laugh or think. It's quite apparent your listeners are in no mood to think very deeply or exert any more effort than it takes to smoke an after-dinner cigar.

Facing this kind of lethargic audience with little inclination to work very hard, what can you do? How can you deliver your message in the most palatable and digestible form? How can you take your listeners on an entertaining and enjoyable trip, so they will be attentive and enthralled when they reach the final serious destination of your talk?

The familiar organization format—OPENING, BODY, CLOSING—is still one of the most appropriate for an after-dinner talk. Your talk should have a serious theme—the after-dinner audience wants to learn but *also wants to be entertained in the process.* To accomplish this, after-dinner speech strategy demands a light touch that literally pleads for a plentiful supply of illustrative stories. Stories that involve people, stories that are human, stories that have a moral. String your anecdotes together like a diamond necklace, each diamond bright and shiny, each vividly illustrating a slice of life.

The typical after-dinner listener has never quite outgrown his childhood desire to be told a story. Jesus knew this 2000 years ago when He gave His sermons in the form of parables. These were stories which illustrated what He was trying to tell the people. They are as vivid today as they were when first told.

"They say I tell a great many stories," Lincoln observed many centuries later, "I reckon I do, but I have found in the course of a long experience that people are more easily informed through the medium of a broad illustration than in any other way."

An after-dinner speech without stories simply won't hold interest. It would, in fact, be a plum pudding without the plums.

We have already witnessed the impact of *stories which hit close to home* such as the executive wasting his whole morning hopping from one small job to another. Listening to this story, few persons fail to draw a parallel with their own work habits.

We have also seen how interest peaks with *stories of famous people* such as Bishop Sheen, Adlai Stevenson, or Churchill, Stalin, and F.D.R. The latter anecdote was made even more effective because of its humorous slant. Audience interest can also be held with *stories of widely known incidents*—remember the story of Moses leading his people out of Egypt?

Another effective type of story-telling is to talk about *your own personal experiences*. Real-life incidents which have happened to you, your friends, or your organization usually have so much meaning to you that you will have little difficulty bringing them to life for a listener. The explorer who describes his travels, the government official who talks about his years in office, the businessman who describes how his company got started—all these people are speaking about their own personal experiences, from which general lessons about life can be drawn which are meaningful to each listener.

As in all other types of speaking, each after-dinner speaker has his own style, tailored to his own particular personality and experiences. This makes it difficult to generalize. The accomplished after-dinner speaker, however, invariably uses a full range of emotion, from humor to pathos. He holds the audience in the palm of his hand—one minute they are chuckling over an amusing incident, the next reflecting on a serious note, or dabbing away a tear.

Some speakers begin with an amusing story and end on a sentimental note. Just as many others end as humorously as they began. The secret is not in the particular sequence employed, but in the *change of emotional pace*. An after-dinner talk which never strays from one emotional plane quickly empties the banquet hall.

Quite often, the after-dinner audience consists of a mixed audience of wives and husbands. This affords the speaker a unique opportunity to capitalize on the interplay always present between men and women . . . Thurber's famed "Battle of the Sexes." Certain types of humorous stories, for example, obtain far greater response from a mixed audience than they would from either men or women alone.

Note how the following anecdote given by a speaker at a Kiwanis Club Ladies' Nite is slanted to stimulate response from a mixed audience.

"When is the last time you men in the audience have remembered your wife with a bouquet of flowers. If it's been very long, you may end up like a neighbor of mine. He went to his service club and heard an inspiring talk on remembering the little woman occasionally with a box of candy or some flowers.

"He took the message to heart and that night showed up at home with both the candy and the flowers. He rang the doorbell and, when his wife opened the door, handed her the candy and flowers. She took one look and burst out into a flood of tears.

"What's the matter?" he asked.

"Oh," she replied, "I've had a terrible day. The washing machine broke down, Junior fell down the front steps, the doorbell's been ringing all day . . . and now you come home drunk."

The after-dinner speech is a common form of speech business executives are asked to give, affording maximum exposure to individuals outside their own organization. Learn how to deliver your after-dinner messages in an entertaining manner and spread your influence far and wide.

LET'S WRAP IT UP

PULITZER PRIZE WINNING AUTHOR Van Wyck Brooks once wrote,

"A great writer is a great man writing."

Similarly in public speaking,

"A great speaker is a great man speaking."

But to be a great speaker, even a great man must first master the basic techniques—how to *CHOOSE* a topic and *ORGANIZE* a speech, project his *PERSONALITY* and develop *PLATFORM TECHNIQUE*, control his *VOICE*, and *STAGE* the talk.

Speech-making reveals to the audience what a man is and what a man knows—it's an expression of his mind and knowledge, his feelings, his character, and his spirit.

In public speaking, as in other fields of endeavor, there are different degrees of perfection. It's a field where the drive to excel benefits the average as well as the talented person. Even an individual of only average ability can develop an effective, and in many cases, an outstanding speaking style. The important measure is what can be accomplished with the natural gifts possessed by each person.

That is the purpose of this book. To assist you to develop your own speaking style to its greatest potential—a style that will enable you to express yourself far better than before, and with greater impact.

A public speaker's style is his manner of expression —how he thinks, how he acts, what he says, and how he says it. There are as many styles as there are speakers—the majestic tones of Winston Churchill, the evangelistic fervor of Billy Graham, the eruditeness of Adlai Stevenson, the folksiness of Will Rogers, the witticisms of Bob Hope. All unique styles, each effective in its own way.

Your style should be distinctively *you*. Here are a dozen key reminders to help you mold it:

1. Speak on a subject you know something about— never talk from an empty head. The well-informed speaker acquires a wide knowledge of many subjects.

2. Allow sufficient time to prepare and organize your speech, forming your ideas into a meaningful design . . . and use plenty of illustrative stories.

3. Rehearse the talk at home—even though practice may be tedious and unexciting, it separates the professionals from the amateurs.

4. Talk your speech from notes . . . and keep the notes short.

5. Be ENTHUSIASTIC, be ENTHUSIASTIC, be ENTHUSIATIC!

6. When speaking, don't try to be someone else. Be natural and project the best possible image— yourself.

7. Be friendly. Put a smile in your voice and on your face . . . and always look directly at your audience.

8. Be voice conscious. Talk loud enough to be heard, pause often, and make your speech colorful by modulating volume, pace, intonation.

9. Gesture while you speak, accentuating your remarks by pointing with your finger, holding out your hand, shaking your head. Use your whole body to get the message over.

10. Tailor your talk to audience size, toning down and beefing up your delivery as audience size varies.

11. Know when to stop. The speaker who talks too long wears out his welcome and gains a reputation for windiness.

12. Spare a half-hour to re-read this little book before you give each talk. Every time you speak to a group, your reputation is on trial. Don't ever deliver a speech to any audience that is one iota less than the very best talk you are capable of making.

Those are the essentials, simply stated. The rest is up to you.